W9-DFV-016

Grandpa jokes

Way Terribly Better Than Dad jokes

Grandpa
The Myth

Q: When is your grandpa's bedtime?
A: Three hours after he falls asleep on the couch.

Q: Why did grandpa put wheels on his rocking chair?
A: He wanted to rock and roll!

Grandpa: I used to have an origami business.
Grandson: What happened to it?
Grandpa: It folded!

A grandfather from Broolyn decided to prepare his will and make his final requests.

He told his wife he had two final requests. First, he wanted to be cremated, and second, he wanted her ashes scattered over Yankee Stadium.

"Yankee Stadium!" the wife exclaimed.

"Why Yankee Stadium?" "Then I'll be sure my son visits me once a week."

Q: What's the worst part about being grandpa?

A: You have to sleep with grandma.

Q: Why do Grandpas smile all the time?

A: Because they can't hear a word you're saying!

Q: Why do grandpas count
   pennies?
A: They are the only ones
   who have the time.

Grandpa: "WIGGLE, WIGGLE,
        WIGGLE YEAH!"
Grandson: Grandpa PLEASE
        put your pants
        back on!

Q: When do you know your grandfather is old enough to retire?

A: Instead of lying about his age she starts bragging about it!

Every time I go to a wedding my grandpa pokes me and says, "You're Next" So then every time I go to a funeral with him, I poke him and say, "You're next."

We call my grandpa Spider-Man.
Not because he has superpowers,
he just has a hard time getting
out of the bathtub.

My grandpa started walking
five miles a day when he
was 60...
Now, he's 97 years old, and
we have no idea where the
hell he is.

A reporter was interviewing a 103 year old great grandfather: "And what do you think is the best thing about being 103?" the reporter asked.
He simply replied,
"No peer pressure."

Grandpa: "Look they made a movie about The Smurfs grown up" Son: Grandpa Please shhhhhhh, that's Avatar...

A Grandfather who had serious hearing problems for a number of years went to the doctor to be fitted for a hearing aid that would return his hearing to 100%.

The grandpa went back for further tests a month later and the doctor said, "Your hearing is perfect. Your family must be really pleased that you can hear again."

To which the elderly man replied, "Oh, I haven't told my family yet. I just sit around and listen to the conversations.

I've changed my will three-times!"

A young man saw an elderly couple sitting down to lunch at McDonald's. He noticed that they had orde- red one meal, and an extra drink cup.

As he watched, the gentle- man carefully divided the hamburger in half, then counted out the fries, one for him, one for her, until each had half of them. Then he poured half of the soft drink into the extra cup and set that in front of his wife. The old man then began to eat.

His wife sat watching, with her hands folded in her lap. The young man decided to ask if they would allow him to purchase another meal for them so that they didn't have to split theirs.

The old gentleman said, "Oh no. We've been married 50 years, and everything has always been and will always be shared, 50/50."

The young man then asked the wife if she was going to eat, and she replied,

"It's his turn with the teeth."

My dear old grandmother always used to say the way to a man's heart was through his stomach. That's why she lost her job as a cardiac surgeon.

My grandpa said he was built upside down.
He said his nose runs and his feet smell.

What did grandpa and grandma do for fun back in the day?
I don't know.
My 17 aunts and uncles won't answer my question.

My grandpa is 95 years old, and he doesn't even have glasses. He drinks straight from the bottle.

My grandpa tried to warn everyone that the Titanic was going to sink. When everyone just ignored him, he yelled at them three more times. Eventually, they got irritated and kicked him out of the theater.

From where did the sperm whale get its name?
Ask your grandparents.

A boy, his dad, and his grandpa
all hear the same hilarious joke,
laugh too hard and pee
their pants...
Guess you could say it runs
in their jeans!

My grandpa just walked into
my room with a young guy
wearing skinny jeans and
eating avocado toast.
I said, "Who is this guy?"
Grandpa: "This is my hip
replacement."

I told my grandpa before he bit the dust...
Grandpa, that's dirty!

My grandpa would always tell me that when he was growing-up, in rural Texas;
His momma would give him $1 and send him down to the store.
He'd come back with 2 loaves of bread, half a gallon of milk, a carton of eggs, and a pound of pork.
He says you can't do that nowadays, way too many security cameras.

My grandpa's last wish was
that when he died, we convert
his ashes into a diamond.
That's a lot of pressure.

Did you know my grandpa
was part of World War 2?
He killed Hitler.

A kids grandparents visit over the holidays go to church for Christmas Mass.
Halfway through the service the grandpa leans over and whispers in his wife's ear, "I've just let out a silent fart. What do you think I should do?"
The Grandma replies, "Put a new battery in your hearing aid."

My grandpa always says, "When one door closes, another opens."
He was a good man, but a lousy cabinet maker.

Three old men are talking about their aches, pains and bodily functions.

One seventy year old man says, "I have this problem. I wake up every morning at seven and it takes me twenty minutes to pee."

An eighty year old man says, "My case is worse. I get up at eight and I sit there and grunt and groan for half an hour before I finally have a bowel movement."

The ninety year old man says, "At seven I pee like a horse, at eight I crap like a cow."

"So what's your problem?" asked the others.

"I don't wake up until nine."

Two elderly grandparents
from a retirement center were
sitting on a bench under
a tree when one turns to the
other and says:
"Slim, I'm 83 years old now
and I'm just full of aches
and pains. I know you're
about my age. How do you
feel?"
Slim says, "I feel just like a
newborn baby."
"Really! Like a newborn baby?"
"Yep. No hair, no teeth,
and I think I just wet my pants"

What's the difference between a teeter totter on a ranch and a donkey's grandpa?
One's a yee haw seesaw and the other is a hee haw peepaw.

My Grandpa died last week, because we couldn't figure out what was his blood type. But he was a strong man, who never gave up and he kept telling us to be positive till the last moment.

What did the grandpa say to his grandson right before he kicked the bucket?
"Hey do you want to see how far I can kick this bucket?"

Girlfriend: Oh no how am I gonna tell dad I'm pregnant?
Me: Leave that to me
later at dinner
Her dad: *coughs*
        I need water
Me: Oh no! Grandpa needs water!

A couple goes out to dinner to celebrate their 50th wedding anniversary.
On the way home, she notices a tear in his eye and asks if he's getting senti-mental because they're cele-brating 50 wonderful years together.
He replies, "No, I was thinking about the time before we got married. Your father threatened me with a shotgun and said he'd have me thrown in jail for 50 years if I didn't marry you.
Tomorrow I would've been a free man!"

A little boy comes running
Into the room and says,
"Grandpa! Grandpa! Can you
make a sound like a frog?"
The Grandpa says,
"I don't know, why?"
The little boy says,
"Because grandma says as
 soon as you croak, we can
 go to Disneyland!"

I was visiting my son and daughter-in-law last night when I asked if I could borrow a newspaper.
"This is the 21st century, old man," he said.
"We don't waste money on newspapers. Here, you can borrow my Tab."
I can tell you, that fly never knew what hit it...

My grandfather died due to shoddy hospital care.
I wouldn't have minded, but he was only in there to visit my grandma.

A police car pulls up in front of grandma Bessie's house, and grandpa Morris gets out. The polite policeman explained that this elderly gentleman said that he was lost in the park... and couldn't find his way home.
"Oh Morris," said grandma, "You've been going to that park for over 30 years! So how could you get lost?"
Leaning close to grandma, so that the policeman couldn't hear. Morris whispered,
"I wasn't lost... I was just too tired to walk home."

For months, Mrs. Pitzel had been nagging her husband to go with her to the seance parlor of Madame Freda. "Milty, she's a real gypsy, and she brings the voices of the dead from the other world. We all talk to them! Last week, I talked with my mother, may she rest in peace. Milty, for twenty dollars you can talk to your zayde (grandfather) who you misses so much!"

Milton Pitzel could not resist her appeal.

At the very nextseance at Madam Freda's Seance Parlor, Milty sat under the colored

light at the green table,
holding hands with the
person on each side.
All were humming, "Oooom,
oooom, tonka tooom."
Madame Freda, her eyes lost
in trance, was making passes
over a crystal ball.
 "My medium... Vashtri," she
  called.
 "Come in. Who is that with
  you? Who? Mr. Pitzel? Milton
  Pitzel's Zayde?" Milty
  swallowed the lump in his
  throat and called, "Grampa?
  Zayde?" "Ah, Milteleh?"
a thin voice quavered. "Yes!
 Yes!" cried Milty.

"This is your Milty! Grand–father, are you happy in the other world?" "Milteleh, I am in bliss. With your bubbie together, we laugh, we sing. We gaze upon the shining face of the Lord!"

A dozen more questions did Milty ask of his zayde, and each question did his zayde answer, until

"So now, Milteleh, I have to go. The angels are calling. Just one more question I can answer. Ask. Ask."

"Zayde," sighed Milty, "when did you learn to speak English?"

A man went to visit his 90 year old grandfather in a secluded, rural area of the USA. After spending the night, his grandfather prepared break- fast for him consisting of eggs and bacon. He noticed a film- like substance on his plate and he questioned his grandfather...
"Are these plates clean?"
His replied... "those plates are as clean as cold water can get them so go on and finish your meal."
That afternoon, while eating the hamburgers his grand- father made for lunch, he noticed tiny specks around

the edge of this plate, and a substance that looked like dried egg yolks...
so he asked again... "are you sure these plates are clean?" Without looking up from his hamburger, the grandfather says... "I told you before, those dishes are as clean as cold water can get them, now don't ask me about it any more I'm getting tired of all this questioning!"
Later that afternoon, he decided to go into a nearby town to get some decent food to eat. As he was leaving, his Grandfather's dog lay across the doorway to the outside and it started to growl and would

not let him pass...
"Grandfather, your dog won't
let me out. Without diverting
his attention from the football
game he was watching on TV,
Grandfather shouted,
"COLDWATER, GET OUT OF
THE WAY."

My grandpa was telling me about when he used to hunt tigers.

He said, "this one time I was alone in the jungle when out of the bushes, right in front of me, a huge tiger leaped out suddenly and went RRROOOOAAAAAARRRRR!!!!!!! Kid, you won't believe it, I shat myself."

I raised my eyebrows. "You bet I believe it, I'd have shat myself too if that happened to me."

"That's not what I mean goddamnit, go fetch me some toilet paper."

So a man and a woman get married, the man tells the woman that he's an avid deer hunter.
The woman says "okay, that's fine." Then they get married. After a couple of years the man going out hunting the woman says "I want to go with you. It's a great bonding experience." The man agrees and they go get her certifications.
He puts her in a blind and says "I'll be in this stand over here and if I hear shots, I'll come running."

A while later he hears her
shots ring off *Bang Bang Bang*
He comes sprinting over to
find her arguing with a man.
She keeps screaming
"THATS MY DEER, DONT
TOUCH MY DEER!"
The man says "Miss you can
keep the deer, just let me get
my saddle off it first"

My grandpa has the heart
of a lion...
And a lifetime ban at the zoo.

I'll never forget my grand–
father's last words...
"Stop shaking the ladder
you little shit"

I asked my grandpa why he
put on his glasses to go get
our dinner.
He said he was going to a
contact–less drive thru.

My granddaddy worked in a blacksmith shop when he was a young fella, and he used to tell me, when I was a little nipper, how he had toughened himself up so he could stand the hard work of blacksmithing.

One story was how he had developed his arm and shoulder muscles. As he told it, he would stand outside behind the wood shed, with a 5 pound potato sack in each hand, extend his arms straight out from his sides and hold them there as long as he could.

After a while he tried 10 pound potato sacks, then 50 pound potato sacks and finally, he got to where he lifts a 100 pound potato sack in each hand and hold his arms straight out for more than two full minutes...
Then, he started putting potatoes in the sacks... DOH!

What did grandpa say before he died in the hospital bed? "Boy, could you put my phone on charging?"

My grandpa asked me to pass him his phone but I passed him a calculator, he couldn't tell the difference.

An 80 year old blind man ask his grandson can you grab my glasses.
Then the grandson
say did you get in the flour again?
Grandpa said no it was the weed.

After years of fighting his cigarette addiction my grand-father finally quit
Breathing...

My grandfather had his tongue
shot out during the war.
He never spoke about it.

My great grandpa was
responsible for the downing
of over 25 German aircraft
during the war.
He was the worst mechanic
in the whole Luftwaffe.

My grandfather had come to visit us. As we were having dinner, he told us of his latest exploits in the world of internet.
He said that he couldn't get through the captcha.
We asked him the problem and he told us that he could decipher and write the letters just fine.
But he didn't know how to put the curved lines.

At 98 years old, my grandfather had the body of a 27
year old.
Unfortunately, the police
found it.

Shout-out to my grandfather
Because it is the only way
he can hear

My grandfather gave me the best advice I have ever heard, just before he kicked the bucket:
Always put on steel toes before doing this.

The last words my grandma told my grandfather was "Sweetie, I'll see you in heaven!" Since then, grandpa has been kicking puppies and setting fire to orphanages.

My young grandson called
the other day to wish me
Happy Birthday.
He asked me how old I was,
and I told him, "62."
He was quiet for a moment,
and then he asked,
"Did you start at 1?"

I'll never forget my grandpa's
last words...
"Are you still holding
 the ladder?"

A little girl is sitting on her grandpa's lap and studying the wrinkles on his old face. She gets up the nerve to rub her fingers over the wrinkles. Then she touches her own face and looks more puzzled. Finally, the little girl asks, "Grandpa, did God make you?"

"He sure did honey, a long time ago," replies her grandpa.

"Well, did God make me?" asks the little girl.

"Yes, He did, and that wasn't too long ago," answers her grandpa.

"Boy," says the little girl, "He's sure doing a lot better job these days, isn't He?"

Made in United States
Orlando, FL
10 February 2023

29801134R00029